fear small
LOVE
BIG

fear small LOVE BIG

Published by The Conrad Press Ltd. in the United Kingdom 2022

Tel: +44(0)1227 472 874
www.theconradpress.com
info@theconradpress.com

ISBN 978-1-915494-16-0

Copyright © Andrew D. Harry, 2022

The moral right of Andrew D. Harry to be identified as author of this work has been asserted in accordance with the Copyright, Designs and Patents Act 1988.

All rights reserved.

Printed and bound in Great Britain by Clays Ltd, Elcograf S.p.A

Typesetting and cover design by The Book Typesetters
www.thebooktypesetters.com

The Conrad Press logo was designed by Maria Priestley.

fear small LOVE ♡ BIG

How to survive a chaotic world

Andrew D. Harry RPP PTP

Contents

Dedication	9
Prologue	10
Introduction	11
1 Unalome	12
2 Winter Sun	16
3 Out of Reach	18
4 Eat Drink Work Sleep	21
5 Carousel	23
6 Arrogance	26
7 Breaking the Spell	30
8 Success	33
9 Another Tune	36
10 Chasing Me	40
11 The Screen	45
12 Fractured Narrative	47
13 Identity	51
14 Gravity	57
15 Cosmic Seed	61
16 Beyond Belief	64
17 Qualia	68
18 The Shadow	70
19 Claim Your Peace	80
20 Clarion Call	82
21 Sovereign	85
22 Mountain of Light	88
23 The Diamond Soul	98
24 Vitality	101
25 Merkablah	105

26 Contentment	107
27 The Door	109
28 Crossing the Rubicon	113
29 Out of the Blue	115
30 Pathway	117
31 All by Yourself	119
32 Mindless Meditation	121
33 Alignment	124
34 Superman	127
35 Sacred Lover	130
36 Paradox	132
37 Chocolate	133
38 Welcome	135
39 Wonder	137
40 Gratitude	139
41 Courage	143
42 Abandon	146
43 Faith	149
44 Terminus	150
45 Rise	152
Epilogue	154
Afterword	155

Dedication

*The unbroken chain
of kith and kin,
each loved that I too
might begin.*

Prologue

*"Fear is the cheapest
room in the house.
I would like to see you living,
in better conditions."*

– Hafiz

Introduction

*"Whoever travels
without a guide,
needs two hundred years
for a two-day journey."*

– Rūmī

1 Unalome[1]

The poets and sages of old,
belovedly sold,
the notion that there exists
a plausible connection,
a way to the light,
where after suitable progress,
through appropriate introspection,
we will have become heaven blessed
and our mere temporal lives
will have ended.
We will have transcended
our baser nature
and become physically,
emotionally and spiritually wise
and have realised
that the ultimate prize

---

[1] A symbol that represents the path one takes to enlightenment.

lies on our very own
path to paradise.

A rare few have attempted
to share a path
to this state of priceless detachment,
where for many,
suffering and pain
remain sustained
by the blight of attachment.

If the purpose of the telling
is the response it elicits,
then, when attempts fail,
the teller, some might say,
rests complicit in the great deception
and can only claim success
if the way is accessible
without exception.

Our understanding and experience
share common ground,
and in both thinking and feeling
life's content is found.

Happiness, though,
will continue to be
a fanciful illusion,
until a return

to the primacy of feeling
is our conclusion.

If we continue to operate
in an identity
that remains arrested
in narcissistic deceit,
we will never be truly free.
So, unfasten reliance
on this notion immediately.

What is offered in this book
is an invitation to look
at the precise mechanism behind
the journey to transcend
the mechanical monkey mind
and help you to find
what it is you want.

It is not the font
of all knowledge,
that is true,
but it will go some way
to reveal exactly
what is stopping you.[2]

---

[2] One of the two NLP Magic questions. Espoused in *The Way of NLP* by Joseph O'Connor and Ian McDermott, published by Thorsons, 2001.

> It will also show,
> that before all else fails,
> we can with confidence
> assume that a humble-love[3]
> prevails.

---

[3] *Conversations and Exhortations of Father Zosima* – Fyodor Dostoevsky, The Brothers Karamazov

2 Winter Sun

Winter sun slants off the water
into my eyes.

A seagull cries overhead.

I sit on this bench alone,
miles from home,
knowing I could be
with you instead.

Here on my own,
enslaved to the man,
feeling like an also-ran
in the great scheme of life.

There must be more than this strife!

Day in and day out,
I doubt they would hear me shout,
even at the top of my voice!

Yet, who are they to me?
Perhaps, we shall see?

Moving on then
to more of the same,
day in, day out,
again and again.

There must be more than this!

No way out.

They wouldn't even
hear me shout.

I don't even know
what I'd have to say.

Oh well, here's to the end of another day.

I guess this is just how it is,
but I can't help thinking,
that there must be more
to it all than this?

3 Out of Reach

Disconnected, out of reach,
the beauty that I see,
would still go on if I were gone,
it's just that it wouldn't be seen by me.

Life goes on relentlessly
year on year.
More life to be ended.
I am worn out
by an incessant fear,
so harsh.
If all there is to this
is blood and sweat and worms,
it is hardly a heart-warming thought,
should it be for nought?

All this toil and effort,
what's it for?

Going back to the earth
to sustain more?

More of the same uncaring life.

If I am good, in a way
they have defined,
I will have achieved a life refined.
Yet, if the refinement of all this loss
is yet more loss?

I shan't find a crumb of hope in it,
just more dross.

Toil and effort to carve out this life.

Perpetual moil,
until I merge with the soil,
to spread me even thinner.

Even the worms, that feast on me,
will be eaten by birds
and the birds in turn
will end up
as something else's dinner.

Instead of dreams of more grind,
my goal is to rise above this, to find
a place to soothe my soul.
Whatever that is?

Perhaps, away from this life,
so unkind?

After all, why would I put
myself through more of the same,
yet again and then again?

Through cycles of gloom,
impending, never ending, doom.

I might as well be kind
to myself at least
and end it all!

Not in the vain hope
of achieving some peace,
but to be released
and no longer suffer this shit.

I wouldn't know then
if it were to carry on
without me,
but the pain and my loss,
and this shit,
would be gone.

4 Eat Drink Work Sleep

I am going to do something about this!
I am fed up with this lonely, daily grind.

In order to put my plan together,
I will need to find some time.

I haven't even got the time to think,
just to eat and drink and work and sleep.
I am beginning to act like a sheep.

Baa baa. Blah blah.
Yes sir. No sir.
Three bags full sir.
Back in the groove,
not able to move.

Whirr, fizz, bleep.

The machine goes on
and on and on.
Slowly, suddenly,
all notions of hope
are gone.

Gone.

Back in the groove,
not able to move.

Whirr, fizz, bleep.

Eat, drink, work, sleep.

My own ideas, again,
remain,
in full retreat.

Whirr, fizz, bleep.
Eat, drink, work, sleep.
Whirr, fizz, bleep.
Eat, drink, work, sleep.

5 Carousel

When I was a child
I remember feeling safe
on this noisy, glitzy, fairground ride.

The barrel organ was shrill
and rattled my brain,
yet each time
my turn was over,
I would want to go again.

I used to think
I was very brave,
clambering onto, then riding,
this gilded, hollow, equine slave.

The merry-go-round horse,
painted frame,
locked in place,

frozen expression on its face.
A shiny saddle and solid seat,
with little wooden platforms,
for my feet.

Holding on, for all my life,
to a spiralling, golden pole,
strangely, securely, skewering
this obedient, lurching beast.
The cacophony and commotion,
a gleeful spectacle, was,
for my young soul,
an infrequent, emotional
and welcome feast.

Oblivious to the implied plight,
as round and round,
up and down,
mechanical cams shifted,
the horses lifted and fell
and I would yell
with unfamiliar delight,
as they dropped to complete
each perfectly defined,
galloping stride.

I can though, now, imagine
the hollow, horses straining to leap,
racing, headlong wild and free,

beyond the strictures
of this spectacular, fairground ride.

6 Arrogance

Is it arrogance sublime,
that I have given so much time
and attention
to automatic reactions,
unwanted distractions,
now beyond their prime?

In giving credence
to those thoughts unseen,
I have allowed
my fears to rule the roost,
unchallenged, unfettered,
my faults assumed, dominating.

I have been paralysed,
consumed.

What possible, credible purpose
is being served,
in behaving like I do?

If only I knew
how to change the script!

Just what can I do
to help myself climb
out of this self-imposed crypt
and leave this zoo?

I am though,
slowly,
cautiously, painfully,
becoming aware
of this log in my eye,
that so limits my view.

If only I knew
how to move it aside.
I would no longer have to hide
behind automatic responses,
deployed to protect,
but now only resulting in neglect,
of those I love and who love me too.

I have just got to get out of this zoo.

Piece by piece,
I will unravel this web,
that so grieves my heart
and confounds my head.

I have decided that
the only thing left to do,
right now, is to work out
how to start.

I haven't a clue what to do,
nor even how to begin.

After all, what do I know,
mere mortal that I am?

My only friend is my deep,
unavoidable, cleansing grief,
which has not yet offered
even a crumb of relief.

All my hope is gone.
What to do?

To get out of this zoo?

I wish I knew[4].

---

[4] 'It may be that when we no longer know what to do we have come to our real work, and that when we no longer know which way to go we have come to our real journey'. – Wendell Berry

7 Breaking the Spell

Turned down a different road today,
on my way to lunch.
Everything seemed so clear.
My head was full of new ideas.
I even acted on a hunch.

I was fitful over the meeting at two.
Then over a tasty chicken soup,
I stepped beyond my usual loop,
of habitual reactions
and emotional distractions,
as I realised it was merely my thoughts,
of what others might do,
that were tying me in knots.

So frightened, I have been,
of my own projections,
of fears, of habitually anticipated,

future rejections.
Now, it is time to stop,
associating certainty with fear
and instead, begin to doubt
the fear itself, when it sticks its head out.

I choose to be certain instead,
certain of something,
of anything else,
but not, for once,
the commanding, demanding,
ever expanding,
fears in my head.

I have been so overwhelmed,
by this dominance of fear,
that it has begun to become
abundantly clear,
that what I think I hear,
this sound of the pounding of dread,
is not, really, real at all.
It is all in my head!

So, at long last I am going to choose
to break the spell I have cast
and choose to be certain instead.

Certain?

Certain of what?

Well, certain of anything,
but that fear in my head.

8 Success

Everyone else tells me what to do,
to think and do and be.
They tell me how I must act
in order to succeed.

To be successful, in this life,
thus, would prove so fruitless, a chore!
Why, would I want to succeed more,
at satisfying a hidden man's need,
just because he or she can shout
and drown everyone else out?

Telling me what to think,
to eat, to drink, to love and hate.

How did I get in this awful state?

This state where I do
as the hidden man pleases.

'Do as 'he says' and you will be fine.
You will have what you want
and be free of diseases.'

To work some more and ruin my health?
At least I will be on the road to wealth!

Yeah sure!

Lining someone else's pockets,
whilst surviving.
When I could be thriving, a-living.

Sitting here writing and reflecting
upon this dross,
all I can feel is a sense of loss.

This doesn't tie in with what I have been told:

'Work hard, do as 'we say' and the streets
will be paved with gold.'

Spending all my time focussing on someone
else's definition of success
and I will have all that I want!
Instead? I get less!

If what I want is defined, by someone else,
with changing needs, why should I bother?

As soon as I reach the next level
there's another and another.

If only there were another door,
that wasn't apparent before?

Still, a few more strides and I'll be there.
At a place that is always
being redefined, by somebody other,
that routinely perplexes my mind
and remains, always, just out of reach.

9 Another Tune

Well, well, what a day.
What is this I say?
'I couldn't possibly, definitely not!'
The chains are released
and out they trot.

What to do with them when they reveal,
the opportunity to heal?

I can choose to take hold of them
and turn them round.

Initially this may sound
clumsy, out of sync,
yet, each time I notice,
I can stop and drink
them in, until they begin
to sing another tune.

I can follow each thread
wherever it leads,
to new expressions,
unseen needs.

Gradually, I can begin to feel
the opposite of each might
be just as real!

What then?
I ask, as I start to flow.

What do I want?

Only I can know!

Yes, only I can know,
what I want to say or do,
to act[5] and express myself,
as I take a step along a brave new road.

I can cast aside ideals,
imposed by others,
I have held in positions
of misplaced authority.

---

[5] Inspired by the book *Life is Tremendous* by Charles 'Tremendous' Jones, wherein 'whatever you believe, act as if it is true' challenges each of us to wrestle with the nature of belief.

They cannot feel what I can feel,[6]
nor know what it is I need.

I must trust myself,
for I am unique
and the universe relies
on the dreams I seed?

I can seed those dreams
and nurture them well.
I can release myself
from the bonds that hold.

I have no need to doubt,
but can choose to be certain,
to be bold.

I need, now, merely, hold
my attention on what I choose,
what it is I want to feel,
and choose to feel it, again and again,
as my doubts retreat.

I can sense what it is to be certain
and discern what it is I need, I have,
I want, I feel and am.

---

[6] Relating to the monumental publication that is *A Course in Miracles*, by Helen Schucman, published in 1976. A year-long study of daily affirmations. A challenging and transformative read.

Each time I take stock and know,
that, even though,
each seems a tiny step, towards a distant star,
in no time at all, the mighty bounds
they have become,
reveal that I have travelled far.

To the growing edge[7]
of the universe and back.

To share what I have learned.

To coax and cajole another soul,
to know they too won't get burned.

When, they leave the surface
of their moon
and plunge into the depths
of their sun.

---

[7] Doctor Randolph Stone, the founder of Polarity Therapy used this term 'the growing edge' to define our journey to challenge and push back our boundary conditions. Set out in two volumes, *The Complete Collected Works* by CLCS Wellness Books, Dr Stone's system is a vast treatise on the ancient modality of Energy Medicine.

10 Chasing Me

I want to change the way I feel.

Now.

Not in some hazy, distant moment.

I have always thought
that I don't know how!

Is somebody else, somehow,
responsible for this,
or is the solution waiting,
hidden within me?

What if I stopped going out
and instead went more fully in?

Will the echoes[8] of my wounds
still chill my soul?

Or could they quietly, gently,
start to sing another tune?

Some help, as my efforts converge,
assists the free flow of energy,
provides a breakthrough,
that brings clarity.
Connections begin to appear,
obviously.
Is this an ancient opportunity?

Am I free to, simply, create a choice,
to find the courage,
to know what is my truth
and end my dependence on
another's view?

With compassion, I can now choose
to tread my own path,
after what has seemed
such a long time,
residing under the yoke
of another man's dreams?

---

[8] 'Unexpressed emotions will never die. They are buried alive and will come forth later in uglier ways.' – Sigmund Freud

It seems,
that I am beginning to believe
that I am ready, to choose
to exercise my power,
through action and expression
in each moment.

In repeating this process,
I have begun, to begin,
to recognise my true nature
and see that now in others too.
Have I found a promising way
out of this zoo?

In knowing what it is I want,
I am beginning to be transformed
and able to choose to transform more.
In an endless cycle, involving, evolving,
becoming grounded and certain.
It is my right.

Quickly and effortlessly,
I surprise myself, in my ability
to be more fully me.

As if for the first time
a concept of safety
begins to appear
and it becomes clear,
it has been, and is,

always here and now,
above and below,
within and without.

There is no need to further suffer
any lingering trace of doubt.

As I start to take my first,
final, faltering steps
along the road to becoming whole,
I need not now assume
that the road is arduous and long,
but can entertain the thought
that I might just be delightfully wrong.

With patience and attention
I notice my rigid, inner shadows,
more readily, start to move.

Manifesting wholeness through
the mere embodiment of love.

First ascending, then descending,
I know that love is here to stay.

It cannot go away.

Though fleeting, it is kindled
and remains eternal.

I embrace it.

I know there is no need to chase it.

For it is impatiently chasing me.

11 The Screen

Awareness may be seen
as a screen[9]
on which all my thoughts
and ideas are projected!

So, what is the source of this screen,
that so intimately observes
all the facets of my life,
yet sits there for so long,
undetected?

Instead of waiting lifetimes then
to discover what lies
beyond the sand, the sea and sky,

---

[9] The Hindu concept of jnana yoga, vichara (self enquiry) as explored in David Godman's book *Be As You Are*, published by Penguin; reissue edition March 7, 1991.

I can surely first try
to seek to find
this screen that lies unseen
behind the unfathomable
labyrinth of my mind.

It seems to me
that this obscure horizon could be
the very source of my being.
Now, that would certainly be
exceedingly freeing,
if true!

12 Fractured Narrative

Forget what the man says!

What is it I really want?

Well, since I was young,
it has been on the tip of my tongue,
but I still don't know where to start.

I've hardly even given it
a moment's thought,
as the man has had all my attention,
my effort, my sinews, my heart.

I suppose what I really want,
is to know what it is I need.

That's a beginning, a seed.
If ever so tenuous.

Yet, why not?
Everything else is becoming
so bloody strenuous.

I need to sleep in and rest,
get things off my chest,
take some time to define,
what is important to me
and what it is I believe.

What have I learnt from this so far?

Well, I have listened
to everyone else for a start!

From now on I think I will take heed
of myself and my heart.

If I think about it,
there is night and day, black and white,
up and down, dark and light.
I wake and sleep, may live and die.

There is in and out, below and above.
There is beginning and end. Loss and gain.
Hate and love.
There is different and the same.

There is hot and cold.
Having an opinion and being told.

There is high and low, push or pull.
There is half empty or half full.

There is hard and soft, and Sun and Moon,
future and past, too late and too soon.

It seems to me that in the world I can see,
there are always two sides to each story,
though the prevailing view
only ever presents just one side
as the road to glory?

If the man says 'this is right',
then, based on my experience,
it's surely, quite possible,
that what he, or she, says is shite?

It is, after all, only one part
of the picture.

So, I guess, at this juncture,
I will have to explore
this a little more.
As, I am sure,
that even to dwell
in the neutral space between,
risks conjuring a notion
of extremes.

An energetic bridge, I assume.

Though it would be wise to be wary
of being snared, or even consumed,
in a concept of opposites
that, by definition,
and without great care,
may further, sustain the fragility
of these mindful conditions.

Nonetheless, to meet [10]
in this field would indeed,
be very neat.

---

[10] 'Out beyond the ideas of right doing and wrong doing, there is a field. I will meet you there' – Rūmī

13 Identity

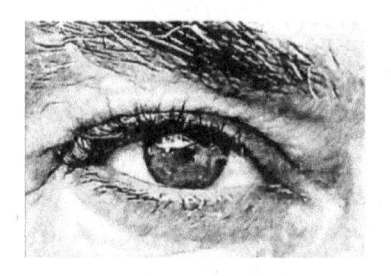

Enough of this!

I know there is more.

I know it at my very core.

What it is I want to find,
lies behind
the fractured screen
of my mind.

It is the certain, ground of being
that lies beyond the dimmed
and intoxicating[11] veil
of my seeing.

---

[11] 'I was never addicted to one thing. I was addicted to filling a void within myself, with things other than my own self.' – Young Pueblo

I choose now to change
the way I deal
with my life,
once again, as I realise,
that rabid corporations
and ambitious men,
relentlessly and ruthlessly, exploit
the very nature of my mind
to polarise.

Carelessly, wielding
the sceptre of stolen, sovereign power,
their misguided manipulation
and my over-reliance on thought,
have effectively wrought
the equivalence of nought,
vicariously.

With breath-taking temerity,
in deploying such fake sincerity,
they are hell-bent on destroying
our culture and now fragile society.[12]

This phantom of phenomena
that so distracts and conceals
and forges a tempting,

---

[12] John Hamer – *The Falsification of History (and Science)* published by Rossendale Books

endless path to my mind,
so supposedly real.

Relentless, in its drive,
in pursuit of the prize,
the germ of consent,
thus generated,
damns all to
karmic servitude.

This will persist,
until we get real,
resist and step off
the peddled wheel
of avarice and greed
and take heed
of what another might need.

To renew this broken frame
and reclaim
our sovereignty,
we need only remember
once again, consciously,
how to feel.

Let me be clear,
there is neither nostalgia
nor effort here.

In feeling, I can simply find my way
and make a fresh, new, certain start
and in every moment of every day,
a tinge of certainty, suddenly,
surprisingly, begins to hold sway.

It is now assuredly,
and abundantly, clear to me,
that I can only truly know
what it is to be real,
when I feel it
in the neglected chambers
of my heart.

The exhaustive, effort
of retreating to the veil behind
my vulnerable and incorrigible mind
can now be left behind,
as it laboriously continues
its computational task.

A conceptual simulation?
A clever algorithm?

Designed, to compare and contrast,
on its arduous, unending,

ultimately disappointing,[13]
solitary and limiting quest?

Just-in-time, this illusory identity,
this great deception,
this awareness of awareness,
The Emperor's New Self,
can be returned, ready for use,
at a moment's notice,
onto the tool shed's shelf.

As I embark on a journey,
so potent and profound,
in a state of clarence[14]
that conjures a feeling,
akin to the warmth
from a curled up, drowsy kitten,
nestled comfortable and safe,
purring upon on my breast.

Wherein, my simmering,
true potential, my very soul,

---

[13] Inspired by the book *Krishnamurti and the Unity of Man* by Carlo Suares, published in 1982 by Chetana, wherein Krishnamurti describes the moment when we become finally and fully disappointed by the mind.

[14] Both a horse-drawn carriage with a clear glass front and the heir apparent within the British Monarchy – A Sovereign travelling with clarity!

can quietly be found,
beyond the maelstrom of my mind,
where it has lain patiently waiting,
deep within the comfort
of my chest.

14 Gravity

Despite the mind's capacity
to contrast and distract
my attention can now
settle on a centre,
of unequalled precision.

Where a certainty of self
resides and replaces
the mind's disappointing,
peripheral, though nonetheless
useful, vision.

As if emerging from a mystical haze,
I am now shielded from
the Medusa's murderous gaze.

With ease embedded,
I know with conviction, exactly,
where my attention is headed.

Regardless of my condition,
I am free, now, to move
through a lens of deepening love.

As silk flows over steel,
there is no need to resist,
but to simply feel my best,
and know what it is now
to truly be real, to exist.

As I feel it, I can, then,
choose to feel it, even more.
Slowly, deftly, subtly,
I approach a deeper, different,
though essentially, familiar shore.

Ceasing to struggle,
I float to an inner, sacred isle, [15]
no longer shrouded in mist.
I can tarry, on solid,
certain ground, a while.

---

[15] The Circum-punct – a symbol of the soul. The dot (soul) within the circle (world).

Transformed, the once vaguely sensed,
dozing feline stirs,
from its mythical slumber,
unfurling a muted, though leonine, roar.

As I choose to feel it,
I can choose to feel it even more.

Ever deeper, fractally, repeatedly,
to my very core.

Then every day, in every way,
I am a mere choice of letting go away.

I now relish the opportunity
to learn to relax more deeply,
until once again I reach
that content-free point,
where heart and soul are understood,
for good.

Without constraint, I free-fall within
and then, as if mastering
some latent, internal gravity,
I accelerate inwardly, repeatedly.

Each time more focussed, yet less intense.
Each time I lose myself I find myself more.
Each time as I feel there is less pretence.

Each time refining in crystalline surety.
Each time less alone and more at home.

Like a life re-born. A new beginning.
With each cycle, I know I am winning
the race to the centre, to my very self.

>At this centre and at
>the growing edge of all,
>I stand, a part.

>Afraid, no more
>and consciously
>grounded in my heart.

15 Cosmic Seed

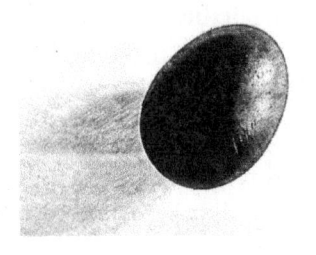

My mind, wide-awake
and aware of itself,
is left reeling, as I realise
that *I cannot think this feeling.*[16]

A feeling of such depth and scope,
that lies beyond the mindful dichotomy
of fear and hope
and the utility of effort and strife.

It opens me to the whole
where I find resides my soul,
the very purpose of my life.

---

[16] With reference to the registered trademark of Heart Enterprises – You can't think a feeling.

My well-practiced need
to control,
born of anxiety and fear,
has inevitably, eventually,
led me here.

Where even now I often try
so hard to control what I see
or what I think is happening to me.

I have unintentionally
gone to some extraordinary lengths
to test my strengths.
I have endured, physical,
emotional and spiritual pain,
without a jot of detectable gain.

This clever cul-de-sac
has dependably, served
as an existential trap.

Yet now, in this more intimate place,
the less I try to seize control
the more certain I become.

The closer I am to home.

I am blessed.

So, relax and know that you, too,
can recreate the conditions
to make a simple choice,
to either think or feel.

A simple, yet apparently
difficult decision, to truly,
enduringly, certainly be real.

Where there is no volition,
nor conditions, no opinions,
nor grievance, no difference,
nor preference,
no hope, nor fear,
no now, no here.

Relax, feel better, enjoy life more.

Refresh yourself.

Drink it in.

It is easier than you think.

In this conscious awareness
find the order that leads,
to the source of your essence,
the cosmic seed.

16 Beyond Belief

My mind wide-awake
and aware of itself
is still reeling,
in the realisation
that consciousness is best accessed,
not through perceptive thought,
but from a simple feeling.

For all my life it seemed to me,
that the world was solely,
defined, sensorily.
I had assumed that
these sensory filters
deliver, to me,
all that there is to think
and sense and see.

In believing thus,
like a little wooden boy,
who within himself,
devoid of any sense of joy,
an empty shell,
has woven, programmed even,
his own limiting, personal spell [17]
and alone has created
a unique kind of hell.

I had naively, and meticulously,
refined my own magic potion,
to suffer and to ensure
that I have remained
a mere isolated drop
in this vast ocean.

Frightened, out of balance
and at times unsettled,
I have still often tried so hard to find
what, I think, will bring me peace of mind.

The more I have tried to identify
with all I that I think I sense and see
the more I fall apart.

---

[17] Wetiko – American First Nation notion of 'mindblindness' as a virulent, psychic pathogen that insinuates thought-forms into one's mind which, when unconsciously en-acted, feed it, and ultimately kills the host.

I only now ever get it together
when I simply remember to feel
deeply within my heart.

I have tried and tried
to think myself out of this place,
but with ever greater effort,
the available space,
in my head,
gets less and less
and I must confess,
that the problem is only ever solved
when I give up my need to control
and instead, accept
that all I need do is to feel,
to let go.

I am also moved to say
that it has come as some relief
to find a simple way to move
beyond balance and belief,
where the deeper I now go,
the more I feel, how far I reach.

In opening myself to the exposure,
of a new-found confidence and composure,
I now aspire to dwell in a certain centre
that has its own deft pull,
which guarantees a feeling
that is peaceable, calm and full.

Like comfrey is nourished
from the earth,
radically, grow deeper
into your certainty
and know your worth.

Trying to think this feeling
is an impossible task.
It is simply madness,
so please don't ask.

17 Qualia[18]

The sun-baked soil reflects
a portion of its heat
onto my warming skin.

My eyes squinting limit
the intense light of day.

Buzzing and swishing,
sounds of wings,
deftly fill my ears,
as the air rises and rushes
around me in its playful dance.

No matter how intensely
I strain my eyes to see,

---

[18] A quality or property as uniquely perceived or experienced by a person.

the fragrance of the blossom
eludes me.

Without volition on my part,
the vital oil bursts into scent.

The heady note created,
completes its unlikely journey,
momentarily, imparting
its joy.

18 The Shadow

This will alarm you,
because it is true.

Our world has been corrupted,
deceptively disrupted,
and our collective wealth hoarded
by those who deploy
some very skill-fully worded
and complicated lies.

Our common lore
has been stolen
through statutory decree
by a few who eschew
what is important
to you or me.

They care for nothing
but service to self,
regardless of the impact
on another.

Contaminating all we hold dear,
feathering their own
luxurious nests,
creating systems of anxiety
and fear
that serve,
solely,
their own interests.

Incessant gas-lighting,
by a complicit
and malignant media,
casts a shadowy pall
over us all,
as they ply
their evil trade,
preying on the innocent
and ignorant,
held in a heartless system,
they have made[19].

Through a mundane dialectic
they spread

[19] *The Psychology of Totalitarianism* by Mattias Desmet

their global infestation,
their pollution,
through the
conventional, sadly familiar, process of
problem, re-action, solution.

Poisoning our soils,
our skies and our seas.
Compromising our health
and spreading distress and disease.
Intent on bringing us
to our knees,
anyway, anyhow, they can.

One rule for them
and one rule for the other,
intent only on the suppression
of the very spirit of man.

In their perversion,
they promise the earth,
but through
persistent inversion,
they deliver nothing
of any real worth.

To be true,
these few
have experienced considerable
material success

in developing an impression
of the widespread normality
of wholesale distress.

Such a shame, then,
when you imagine
what they could have achieved,
if they weren't so stunted
by what they have chosen
to believe.

Caught, with their hand
in the global cooky jar,
they would, of course, go too far
and press for a truth
and reconciliation commission.

Whilst true to form,
and with a slick, sleight of hand,
these worms would,
more likely, stealthily mobilize
another brutal inquisition.

The audacity and scale
of their wholesale greed,
and insatiable, infantile need,
has, so far, come
at our collective cost.
So much so, we are all hurting now.

Although, believe me, all is not lost.

There is a simple remedy.

These wretched, degenerate souls
have an Achilles' heel, it seems?

A lack of imagination limits their aspiration
toward what being human really means.

In compensation, they are hellbent
on augmenting a version of reality
only they think they understand.

Frightened of their own mortality,
as they invest in their arbitrary rules
and illusory mansions of sand.

We can send a message
and end the societal friction,
that has resulted
from the identification
with an unlawful, legal fiction.

A heresy of hearsay,
perpetuated through
cultivated, confusion
and cunning misdirection.

We can seize the option
to end this co-option
to victimhood
and remember that we
are universal entities,
expressing ourselves
as flesh and blood.

We are sovereign, not slaves.

Grounded thus and standing
in our inherent power
we can shrug off the bestial stench
of this putrid shower
and in our glorious humanity
awaken to delicious, refreshing sanity.

We need not be so controlled
by such limiting convention,
but are at liberty to be creative
and set the intention
to return to a simple,
wholesome, organic creed,
on which we can all be agreed.

We can organize society,
without the stolen authority
of bloated, tyrannical,
governing bodies, and
collectively accept again

the natural law, in which enough
of us live to first do no harm.

This would generate and perpetuate
a widespread effect for the common good,
that, on a societal scale, would transform
and reset our cultural norms,
like a charm.

Let us, thus, foment
a mass consent,
to be exact, to treasure
with equal measure,
the value of each sovereign self
and naturally, consistently
accept and enact
the familial 'law of we',
one and all, as a community.

With common-purpose re-framed,
we can fluently declare
notice to reclaim
our inalienable rights,
resolving outward chaos
inwardly and gladly,
embracing our responsibility.

Where, when we digress,
and our standards fall,
through action or inaction,

we must eagerly invite
effective redress
and proportionate sanction,
delivered through trust
in, and the appreciation of,
the informed consideration
of our esteemed peers.

As a result of such
a burgeoning fifth column
of love and respect,
the subversive cult,
we have seen through the years,
would yet, quickly disappear.

Such unity would instil robust immunity
to their crude, cruel tool
of divide and rule.
With no place to hide,
the demonic and fetid tide
would rapidly subside.

Replaced, on the whole,
by a service to soul,
we the people, will eventually succeed,
through the law of equity,
in releasing the shackles
of this aged tyranny.

Rightly, again free.

Free to breathe, free to smile,
free to tarry a while.

Free to laugh, free to frown.
Free to be up and free to be down.
Free to be stop and free to grow.
Free to come and go.

Free to rest and free to earn.
Free to ignore, free to learn.
Free to think and free to speak.
Free to eat and free to drink.
Free from fear and free from hunger.
Free to expect and free to wonder.

Free to settle and free to excite.
Free to have a private life.
Free to celebrate and free to protest.
Free to be serious and free to jest.
Free to work and free to play.
Free to listen and free to say.

Free to be held and not restrained.
Free to argue and free to resist.
Free to agree and free to assist.
Free to start and free to desist.
Free to be meek and free to be bold.
Free to let go and free to hold.

Free to dislike and free to respect.
Free to learn and free to forget.
Free to separate and free to connect.

Free to follow, free to lead.
Free to speak, free to hear.
Free to counter, free to cheer.
Free to be confused and free to be clear.

Free to act, free to rest.
Free to be your worst and be your best.
Free to offer and free to accept.
Free to confirm and free to correct.
Free to provide and free to care.
Free to give and free to share.

Free to stay and free to move.
Free to embrace and free to love.
Free to know when
enough is enough.

19 Claim Your Peace

In your whole life,
have you ever known
a moment without fear?

Well, draw near,
for I have a tale to tell.

It may well come as some surprise
that the mechanical mind cannot
reprise the solution,
but will certainly continue
to deliver ever more light pollution.

Let it do its job,
it is not here to rob
your soul,
but to help you achieve
your earthbound goal.

There is no point waiting
for the conflict to cease.

To win this war,
you must first
claim your peace.[20]

---

[20] Inspired by a conversation in an episode in series one of *Star Trek Discovery*, a Netflix Original Series, 2017.

20 Clarion Call

I have stumbled upon
the answer to a question
I had not thought to ask
and have now unwittingly unmasked,
a folly of epic proportions,
that still sustains, on occasion,
limiting, mindful,
projections and distortions,
which obscure a powerful truth.

In learning to let go,
we can describe consciousness
and awareness
as two distinct things,
according to this kinaesthetic sleuth.

The latter, you will find,
sustains a perpetual toil
in your mind.

The former, a feeling
where the sky has no ceiling,[21]
where mere ideas of love
form but pale imitations
to the ease found
through relaxation.

A simple step it is,
that helps you to change state,
and enables you to vitally,
re-calibrate.

Know this and you and your soul
will never again be,
seemingly, parted.

You will have become lionhearted.

So, let an inner, heartfelt roar
well-up and send a clarion call
far and wide,

---

[21] Beautifully articulated in the song 'Audition (The Fools Who Dream)', from the Original Motion Picture Soundtrack of *La La Land* 2016.

to invite one and all,
to join the pride.

21 Sovereign

I do not answer questions.
I don't understand legalese.

I am sovereign, a man of the land,
flesh and blood, heart and soul.

So please,
resist the urge to confuse me
with some legal fiction,
conjured up by some
well-meaning fools,
unwittingly co-opted
to play their part,
as convenient tools,
in a vast deception.

You are, to be frank,
out of your jurisdiction.

I stand under a common lore.

One shared by all, owned by none
and superior to all others.

Where, to do no harm,
is the only rule.

Yes, the only one.

I have a personal contract
divinely inspired,
where all that is required,
is that I cause no loss to another,
nor commit no fraud
toward my sister or brother,
and keep the peace as I journey
through this beautiful day.

I have no interest
in contracts you may think
you have made
and will not assist you
to assert what you believe
to be your authority.

For in the grand scheme of life,
it is we the people
who are the majority.

Let us keep this a civil matter
and I thank you for the kind offer,
but there is no consent,
no contract, nor joinder here.

Of the many choices
I might make this day,
I will be selecting another.

Unless you wish to impede
my travel along
my chosen path today,
may I suggest,
with the utmost respect,
that you step aside
and I will be on my way.[22]

---

[22] Precedent: Rice versus Connolly 1966 & UCC 1-308

22 Mountain of Light

Approaching the summit,
through a path hewn from rock,
lies the Heaven's Gate.
Where is found a majestic hall
with polished black and white
marble floors
and intricately carved
columnar walls.

High above, a crystal ceiling,
clear to see.
Supported by an exquisitely
forged, gilded frame,
looks out onto a blazing night sky.

Here, mesmerised
by the grandeur of the space,
it is disappointing that I can look out

on this vast beyond, yet,
it will not yield to my touch.

Time barred, I can see,
that to reach my home in the stars,
I need to find another way
not previously evident to me.

Perhaps, through a more personal
and complete cosmology?

This glorious, yet vacuous
and impersonal palace,
devoid of anything,
but a mere temporal value,
alludes to an implied purpose.

A treasure? Per chance,
or maybe a chalice?

I seek the barely sensible
in the chill, wintry gloom.

Ahead, steps ascend
to an altar-like platform.

I spy a shadowy gap,
some way off to my right.

How far?

It's difficult to measure.

Clutching at straws, I set off,
intrigued.

Imagination fuelling anticipation.

Closer now, but not much clearer
a cleft emerges as I edge nearer.

Before me grey still forms.
Impressions only, nothing certain.

Slowly, gingerly pressing forward.

My open hands reach out before me.
Finger-tips touch, a shiver spreads.

I recoil.

Velvet?

Heavy, dense, beautiful fabric.
Curtains of red!

Parting them reveals nothing,
but cool scent from spring flowers,
carried on a zephyr beckoning me
from below.

Instinctively, I reckon,
I should follow.

Taking one cautious step,
reverentially, repeatedly,
I proceed.

I feel my way in the dark.

Tight steps rotating down, just my size.
A helical staircase is revealed,
descending clockwise.

Carefully, trusting this hidden master's craft, and without
a backward glance,
I disappear gingerly, timorously
into this obsidian shaft.

Dazzling darkness
and deafening silence,
tempered by the delightful breeze,
accompany my slow, steady progress
down and around.

Reassured by the rhythm of my breath,
and my feet,
my initially, impetuous belief,
is persuaded into faithful adherence,
with the renewed promise
of each reliable stride.

How far now?

I am not sure,
but there is surely more?

One step and then another.

Just what will I discover,
or what might I miss,
as I spiral further down
into this abyss?

Inevitably, the pace is slow,
as step by, careful, step I go.

Steady and sure.

Cautious and attentive.

I find that I develop
more trust in this process,
though visually compromised.

Foot falling echoes resound,
reverberating, changing,
each time around.

Progress?
I am not sure, if there is more?

Patience tested, senses rested,
coiling down, deeper still.

This darkness, now familiar,
becomes comforting, real.

In this womb-like space,
I start to relish the reliance
on something else
and notice a shift
in how I feel.

Each turn repeats,
giving way to yet another.

Further down and around
relying only on breath and touch
and sound.

Without the filter of my eyes,
I start to sense things differently,
through a new type of light.

I stay in this light feeling, persisting,
though now growing agitated,
disturbed.

Fearful thoughts seep through
to my mind,
erratic and perturbed.

Not yet panic,
but close I know.

I am anxious though.

A tiger's tail, tentatively held!

I stay with it and continue,
warily, down and around.

Stay with it, now. Stay with it.
Down and around.
Down and around. Stay with it.
Down and around.

My fretful frenzy at its peak,
Resigned now, I release
the long, imaginary, caudal form.

Directly, my descent stops,
replaced by welcomed and solid ground.

I settle to sit. Now silent and still,
upon warm, dry, firm earth.

Resting, catching my breath.
I sit and rest some more.

Eventually and unexpectedly
there settles on me a sharper,

gentler, more refined, delightful
and certain, sense of self-worth.

Perceptibly, my life-purpose,
instantly, now clear to me.
The heavens above,
intimately near to me.
Each element,
intrinsically, part of me.

Firmly centred in this safe harbour,
free from the need of more labour.
A sense, of intense, easy focus.

Contentment.

In union now.

Like Samadhi.[23]

I rise and walk with such ease.

Confidently and calmly, without a care,
I return outside to sing to my trees.
They know me.

---

[23] A state of meditative consciousness, the final stage, at which union with the divine is reached (before or at death).

Embracing and inhaling
the fresh, evening air.

I am surprised by certainty.

Like a day lent from summer,
when the song begins to sing itself.[24]

Nothing lost, everything regained.

I carry within me a new-found clarity,
framed in a feeling, that assures me
that this very personal sanctuary
is always directly, accessible to me
and directly, accessible to one and all.

Now more intimately familiar
with the scope of my bodily form,
I find, I am no longer, personally,
defined by it!

Though I accept, that, for many
this, may yet,
seem to still be the norm.

Instead, I can now appreciate
this perfect vehicle, primed,
maybe even designed,

---

[24] Poem of William Carlos Williams, American Poet, 1883–1963.

to help me experience a state
that is so much more refined
and that enables me to travel
with clarity and certainty,
along, what was before,
an unknown, inaccessible road.

One that leads,
delightfully,
toward an entirely,
more eternal,
even spiritual,
abode.

23 The Diamond Soul

Along the road to becoming whole,
lies the building of the diamond soul.

Mist hangs thick and cool.

The sun's rays elicit warmth
for the new day.

Rivulets of myth and bliss
flow along the growing edge
of the emerging dawn.

Rose and lily, on window-ledge,
scent the air.

Light streams on dreams and industry there.

A knowing smile breaks out
on all who enter
this establishment of presence.

It is a place to ground
and truly connect
to this hectic world
of black and white
and the illusion
of wrong or right.

To fuse with love another way
and balance impulse gone astray,
to clear the path to harmony.

Where what I need is what I feel,
it is what I want and have.

I am the link to parity
and a simple law of love.

Now is the time to be myself
and to move with clarity.

To build upon foundations tested
by gracious hearts and loving hands,
I have rested.

No longer whether, but now when,
without as within, the time is nigh.

My feet touch the earth,
my head the sky.

I am in my element.

Home at last,
now I am able,
to express and to involve,
to bustle and hustle
and take my place
to nourish from my table.

Without compromise or dilution,
I will act on my own terms.

I'll take no truck and pass no buck
for there is work to do.

Until subject and object are one,
when the race will have been run,
up the mountain of the Moon,
on our journey to the Sun.

My place can be found
in the building of the diamond soul,
that lies along the road
to becoming whole.

24 Vitality

You may not know,
but for life to exist,
energy must flow
and a balanced state
persist.

According to
universally accepted norms,
energy is never lost,
it merely changes form.

Through observation,
we have learned,
that positive potential
converts to negative
through a neutral field
and then returns.

From north to south
and back again,
it's all very neat.

The cycle occurs
and the circuit is complete.

If this harmony remains
the cycle will repeat,
perpetually.

Any departure from this state
will cause the energy
to dissipate
and the health of the system
to deteriorate.

Recovering this crucial
ambivalence
ensures equity is
once again obtained
and its vitality
reclaimed.

Thus, your energy anatomy
has held you since
before your birth.

An intelligent organisation
of elements,
ether, air, fire, water and earth.

Dynamic, yet stable,
a simple dipole,
affords another opportunity
to mature your soul.

To cradle an electro-magnetic
personality
and, in resonance,
exhaust your skill,
through the sustenance
of a massive act of will.

Life is a balancing act
and you win
the race
when, in a state of ease,
you choose to embrace
your polarities.

Positive, negative,
active, passive,
objective, subjective,
alkaline, acid.

A-living for aeons,
your resilient ions,

simply and surely
know what to do.

If, on reflection,
you can ensure,
that you favour
neither side,
then they will,
for certain,
help you gravitate
toward what is true,
for you.

25 Merkablah

Many seekers do think,
as is widely implied,
that the centre is reached
if the blade is forced up,
directly, to pierce the cup,
only to find
that the grinding pressure
takes forever, sapping strength,
binding the soul, whilst life wanes,
as on an ebbing, spring tide.

Yet, I have found,
when all is said and done,
the longest way round
is the shortest way home
and we can, otherwise,
and with ease,
incidentally, achieve our goal,

when we let the mountain(s) gently,
cascade into the sea(s).

Our bases, thus, loaded
and life force encoded,
in a spiralling expression
of the law of three.

Each a flowing, flooding, flowering,
flourishing, fully formed, star seed.

To truly touch base, it is,
then, perhaps, best
on the seventh day to rest
and to drink from a cup
that fills you up.

Don't you think?

26 Contentment

All is love at inception.

Susceptible to being intercepted
by exceptional deception,
the mind is then seized,
imperceptibly lost in perception.

Thoroughly taken, firmly yoked
by, what is it, a creative engine,
or a cosmic joke?

Where suffering and pain
will surely visit again and again?

As in turn, concepts refine by design,
each time,
unless, and until, receptive

to a contraceptive
for this obdurate mind worm.

The precept?

Unfasten and accept,
a concept-free[25] philosophy,
to identity.

Life is not some perceived ideal,
it is what it is.

Listen, observe, get real.

Relax, feel better, return to love,
as contentment is by far your best move.

Believe me,
to achieve this certainty,
is easier than you can
possibly conceive.

---

[25] 'The description is not the described; I can describe the mountain, but the description is not the mountain, and if you are caught up in the description, as most people are, then you will never see the mountain.' – JD Krishnamurti

27 The Door

Images from lore offer a little more
in our quest, to recover the optimal state
that is our rested-best.

Like a double-edged sword
parries and thrusts,
our binary mind
will compare and contrast,
to keep us fully engaged
to the future and the past
and to stay vulnerable to extremes
and perpetually, shallow
and manipulative memes.

As Icarus teaches us
through his misguided demise,
do not be distracted
by a mere conceptual prize.

To live by it is to die by it,
no matter how well it is wielded.

Instead, listen passively
to free yourself
from this karmic bondage
to remain safely shielded.

To put your armour on,
all you need do,
is take it off [26]
and through this embodiment
you can safely execute
your return from Oz,
because,
only through the act of love
can you touch
the night sky above.

Know that the I knows how,
only you know when,
and there is no why!

Where to start?

---

[26] The simplest description of the epic tale of *Sir Gawain and The Green Knight* by Anonymous.

Rely not on the I of the mind,
but on the I of the heart.[27]

The former, the tree of knowledge,
that sustains perceptual strife,
the latter a gateway to innate happiness,
the very tree of life.

Habitual reliance on
mere thinking must stop,
if you are to become
the divine ocean
within this simply, human drop.[28]

Before flowing out, fully,
we have the key to enter in.
Connected thus, the very universe is ours,
for when the sun sets, only then,
can we see the stars.

Sense it, feel it, trust it, love it
and above all begin.

For, contrary to many popular,
adolescent themes,
this means

---

[27] Proverbs Chapter 3 Verses 5,6

[28] 'You are not a drop in the ocean, but the entire ocean in a drop'
– Rūmī

that the only way out of this,
is in.

A super-position,
where no effort is required.
Simply, choose and be,
inspired.

28 Crossing the Rubicon

There is very fine
and a very distinct frontier
that appears impermeable,
when you have identified
with concepts, created
from a mindful perspective
over your informative years.

Although you may think
that the die has been cast
and the span of your life
has been set,
limits defined,
by the assumed scope
of your mind,
suggest the extent
to which the sweep of your awareness
can plausibly aspire.

No matter how hard you have
tried to think yourself out of the box,
the effort itself, exhaustively expended,
merely piles on more conceptual locks.

To cross beyond the partition,
constructed by your very own mindful volition,
you need only accept that trying won't work and
you can just choose to relax instead.

What opens then before you
and within you,
will astound you,
when you feel its simplicity
and imperious reach.

No need to pause as you step this way
to reclaim the seat
of your sovereign power,
nor worry that you may pass
a point of no return.

Let go and be delightfully surprised
in each and every conscious hour
by what you can now learn.

29 Out of the Blue

Seemingly insulated.

Stumbling, blindly muted.

Bathed in fear.

Constant, inconsistent effort,
ensures perpetual isolation.

Seasoned observation
clashes with concepts
subordinate to direct experience.[29]

---

[29] The pioneer of plasma science 'The Thunderbolts Project' has inspired a new school of investigation called plasma cosmology. It has achieved surprising success in predicting major discoveries through observation.

Healthy, practised imagination
disappoints, despite impressive appearance.

Thoughtful identification
filters eternal fragrance,
further frustrating understanding,
through limited representation.

Misguided, mindful attempts
to storm the gates
render insight impossible,
when all along
the cosmic symphony
remains accessible,
opening with ease,
to a deep and loving surrender,
providing sanctuary to all,
who give in.

Trust instilled, certainty surprises,
igniting inner ambition,
flaming with co-creativity,
seemingly at will.

Obscuring clouds
and illusory blue sky above,
acquiesce, to a sea of stars,
where dark, teeming ocean tides
stream toward love.

30 Pathway

OK, before I go berserk,
tell me, exactly how does
this relaxation gig work?

It is no secret,[30] you must learn
to fear small and LOVE BIG!

It is so simple, that if you blink
you will miss it,
yet it is not what you might think.

From a standing start,
simply, begin to identify,

---

[30] In 'Feeling Is The Secret', Neville Goddard outlines a clear system where the world you experience is a direct result of your level of consciousness.

not with your head,
but your heart.

You will not begin,
to get this until,
you take a step toward it,
if that is what you want.

Your path will only start to show,
when you dispense with what
you think you know
and dwell on someone,
or something you love instead.

Kindle that feeling in your heart,
touching nothing else,
let the warmth from this lamp spread.

A pure flame will then grow
and you will begin to know
more than the mind's filters
can ever reveal.

31 All by Yourself

When you are all by[31] yourself
you feel serene,
there's no need for wealth.
Still silent, cold and clean.
No need to panic.
No need to think.
It's just an antic,
that some people use
to push you over the brink.

You try hard enough,
you're doing well.
No need to bluff.
Good day, farewell.

---

[31] *Reflections on the way to school*, by Robyn Harry aged 11.

I sit here peacefully,
looking up at the misty sky,
the birds fly, gracefully,
wondering why
I was ever left alone.

32 Mindless Meditation

If love's feeling eludes you,
do not be downcast.
It's not the only way
to still the mind and ignite
your own, personal, pilot light.

Simply and deeply, now breathe,
nice and slow.

Slow.

Take some time to settle
and there you go.

In and down. Up and out.
In and down. Up and out.
In and out. In and out.

Focus your attention
at the top of your chest,
as the air flows past.

In and down. Up and out.
In and out. In and out.

Imagine now as you settle,
that this slow, sure current flows gently
through a silken, gossamer, thin web.

Delicately seized, as it progresses.

Momentarily arrested,
the web flutters and fills,
the passing air spills
and you feel its delicate pull.

In and down. Up and out.
In and out. In and out.
Slowly, in and out.

As time passes by, a warming sensation
tenderly, perceptibly, sustains your attention.

This glow spreads and a relaxing, feeling
of warmth, grows within your chest.
Kindle that feeling in your heart,
touching nothing else,
let the warmth from this lamp spread.

In this simple meditation,
patiently wait.

Directly, your love becomes
the purest medication,
the guardian at the gate.

A pure flame will then grow
and you will begin to know
more than the mind's filters
can ever reveal.

No content, nor effort, required.
Just love to relax,
and deeply heal.

33 Alignment

The mind is a very useful tool, for sure.
Yet, it is not who you are.

You are so much more!

Did I mention,
that with balanced attention,
on both cardiac and nervous systems,
you regain a quantum state,
a super-position?

Connected then, both outside and in,
a flow is set up twixt the two
and your intelligent energy starts to spin.

The circumpunct, the circle and the dot,
forms an ancient conjunction.
A 2D representation of what happens now

as you access so much raw information.
In 3D and more the flow goes toroidal,
a portal opens you
to a further dimensional place,
a gate,
far beyond your ideas
of time and space.

For the avoidance of doubt,
you can find this out for yourself,
by going in.

Forgiving both future and past
and learn, at last, poised,
to discern the signal from noise
and see anew,
as your voyages in time[32] continue.

With body-mind,
spirit and soul so aligned,
like Pegasus himself,
you will no longer be
so temporally confined.

When you can again think
and feel in equal measure,

---

[32] Inspired by Kula Shaker lyrics 'How can we see, when we are travelling in time' from the song *Time-worm*.

you will dwell at the threshold
of a wondrous treasure.

Right now, consider
that one genuine, heartfelt moment
is worth a million thoughts.

Accept this, and then repeat,
until mind, body and soul
are coincident, coherent,
whole, replete.

Your return to innocence
complete.

How many lives will it have taken
to let go thus?

Maybe, in due course,
you will know,
but, for now, you must drop
the thought of more jam tomorrow,
in order to consolidate and appreciate
this healthy state,
that is devoid of such mechanical
pain and sorrow.

34 Superman

At his core he is a man of steel.
Here to help you to find
what it is to be real.

Your fretful wanderings,
at dead of night,
reveal the time has come
to kindle a new kind of light.

From the darkness[33] within,
at the very womb of your being
there lies a feeling,
which when nurtured with care,
will transform into a flaming
temple of fire.

---

[33] A shared theme of Camus, Jung and Rūmī.

If you do not aspire to start,
you simply won't find out.

So, learn to relax and feel better.

Don't hide from it,
reside in it,
where there is
no doubt.

Prepare to uncover
that invincible summer,
that has lain dormant
midst the mind's winter,
and let your soul pull
on your heart strings,
as you feel your way
in this dark night.

It is certainly not
what you might think,
for therein lies your fear,
your kryptonite.

Let go, accept
and let it burn
and you will realise,
you will be
more than alright,
and not a little surprised,

as your soul
takes flight.

35 Sacred Lover

There is a deep need to appreciate
how to learn to let go,
to loosen reliance on thinking
and begin again to feel instead.

Yet, even when you have learned
to habitually take as much notice
of your heart, as our head,
external events, can even then,
be so prolonged and intense
that you may again descend
into the clutches of an anxious mind,
seemingly spent.

Remember, you are both magician
and your very own physician
and that the unknown
is your forever home.

Know that you can recover.

Find time to rest and explore.

Listen to your own music.

Be your own sacred lover
and you will discover,
still more.

36 Paradox

I know now,
that before
all hope is gone
and the light goes out,
I can switch off, to switch on,
to be in no doubt.

I am glad I have scratched
this particular itch,
the one where love and fear
don't play on the same pitch.

How do you feel about this?

Do you think
you too will switch?

37 Chocolate

Conscious as I am and at rest in certainty,
as warming chocolate softens
in a bain-marie,
relaxation exposes me
to a contagious love,
that so delightfully infects my life.

Its radiant heat dissolving my loss,
anxiety and isolation.

As I feel my way in the dark,
I open further to this love,
that resides beyond sensation
and defines itself through

the consequences[34]
of my relaxation.

---

[34] Consciously cultivate: calmness, clarity, comfort, contentment, connection, confidence, capability, consistency, composure, creativity, certainty, courage, coherence, congruence, common-sense, compassion, collaboration, clair-cognizance.

38 Welcome[35]

Oh, golden one, vital and bright,
what can be done to shine this new light,
such that it can be seen by everyone?

Simply, attune, feel it in your heart.
Soon, a nourishing flow will start.
This flow will, with patience,
become a flood.[36]
Spirit and soul, conscious and whole,
warms our water and our blood.

Bathe in this glow and you will know
what this life is for.

---

[35] 'Nearly home trees' approaching Cornwall on the A30 West-bound.

[36] 'When you do things from your soul you feel a river moving in you, a joy.' – Rūmī

A blessing for sure.

'Kia Ora.'[37]

---

[37] 'Kia ora' is a warm and welcoming greeting you'll hear throughout New Zealand and comes from the indigenous Māori language.

39 Wonder

This heart-felt sense of self, is love.

It is what we are and everything is
and does not come from above.

Keenly expect it, routinely accept it,
know in your heart that it is there.

In a continuous act of will,
deliberately stand, focussed, still,
within your power.

Gently, effortlessly, and with great care,
embrace and fully appreciate this feeling,
as you lay it all bare.

You will clumsily, impatiently,
want to share

this glittering gem, and bestow
what you now know, this diadem,
to each and every one of them.

As you say, in as many ways
and hope you can be heard,
as well as understood…

'I love, with you.'

40 Gratitude

Axiomatic, practical and fine.

Frequently forgotten,
much maligned.

I would feel perturbed
if this striking gem
were left undiscovered,
undisturbed,
yet again.

I have promised myself
that I will oft lift the lid,
to agitate and ensure
it is lovingly stirred,
this way and that,
in a continuously, apparent
and chaotic motion

to keep it churning in response
to a deep devotion.

Keenly tended, through skill
and focused intent,
it is sensitively tweaked and tested,
then on occasion lavishly rested.

Until, in time,
its way is wended and matured.

Ready to be freed.

Open to the air
and to the light of day.

A savour sublime,
patiently cultivated,
now complete.

When tasted it leaves
its attentive recipient
replete.

Such a vintage fetched
is gratefully appreciated
and with each new delicious sip.

It can be treasured again and again,
and more and more,
just as a wave encounters the shore.

It builds and is beached,
its burgeoning potential
is once more reached,
before it is reclaimed
by deep currents that take it home
beyond this temporal world.

Another spirit unfurled,
elated, elevated, expanded,
not withheld or abated
by the drag of this gross, dreary realm.

On this journey we are,
therefore, contrarily invited,
ergo, to take the helm
and steer a straight course
that requires us to venture
in our own way to find
myriad opportunities to be kind.

Each conscious choice thus,
draws on a deep wellspring,
from our vantage point above.

Each time, we are refreshed,
replenished, our hearts surely,

maturely, becoming more purely,
wedded to love.[38]

---

[38] 'Love is the greatest refreshment in life' – Pablo Picasso

41 Courage

Trust yourself.

You are unique
and the universe relies
on the dreams you seed.

Seed those dreams
and nurture them well.

Release yourself
from the bonds that hold.

Do not doubt. Be certain. Be bold.

Only you can choose
what it is you want,
you need, you feel, you are.

Take stock and know,
that even though
each seems, but a tiny step
towards a distant star,
in no time at all,
the mighty bounds
they become
will reveal that you
have travelled far.

To the growing edge
of the universe and back,
to share what you have learned.

To coax, cajole another soul,
to know they won't
get burned.

When they leave
the surface of their Moon
and plunge into the depths
of their Sun.

Without compromise or dilution,
act on your own terms.

Take no truck
and pass no buck,
for there is truly,
work to do.

Until subject and object
are one,
when your race
will have been run,
up the mountain of the Moon,
on your journey to the Sun.

Your place can be found
in the building
of the diamond soul,
that lies along the road
to becoming whole.

42 Abandon

The curtains were drawn.
The house wasn't warm.
I leant against the back of the chair.
Through the lounge window I stared,
at the world out there
and nobody cared.
Nobody heard me.
Nobody saw me.
I felt lost, all alone,
even though I was at home.

Many years have since gone by
and I pass that window often now,
from the other side.
I recall how it was,
as I peered out
so young and naïve
and I have allowed

myself to dwell
on that haunting scene.

In not turning away
from the aged pain,
I have come to believe
that it has been a gift
to visit this formative event
once again.

Regularly, attentively,
avoiding the urge to run,
I have slowly realized
that instead of being a store
of some suppressed trauma
this frozen scene
overwhelming me
over all these years,
an arid stream
of unexpressed tears
paralysing my life,
can be now and always
could have been,
seen in a different light.

If I were to see it then
as I choose to see it now,
where I know
that with love of self,
I was never truly alone.

Abandonment and shame
are simply now reframed,
a lifetime of recollections
awash with love reclaimed.

43 Faith

It is not absurd to believe,
that the greater I feel it in my heart
and the more certain of self I become,
I will know and trust that we are one.

When, through our actions, we all develop faith in this
simple little rule,[39]
we can all realise
the perfect, pure potential
of Zero, The Fool.[40]

---

[39] Stephen Wolfram's book *A New Kind of Science* explores a fundamental new way of modelling complex systems by following very simple rules. It challenges the dogmatic dominance of mathematics through an exploration of the concept of computational equivalence.

[40] In Tarot 'The Fool' is the most powerful card in the pack, symbolising our pure potential for transformation.

44 Terminus

My intrepid and loyal friend,
at last, we have reached
what appears to be the end.

Our perilous, and perfectly,
challenging journey,
safely made.

Time now for festivities,
singing, dancing, merriment,
to celebrate a testing time,
and in good company,
it was time well spent.

The way we have come,
often uncertain, unclear,
in no time at all is left behind
and familiar and certain ground

we now find.
We can, after all, readily agree,
we are here.[41]

What next?

Well, it has taken such a long time,
what's the rush?

Lean heartily now,
on this, your treasure chest.

Relax deeply,
feel better and enjoy
the rest.

---

[41] *Terminus*: This word comes straight from Latin. In the Roman empire, a *terminus* was a boundary stone, wherever there was a *terminus* there could be no arguments about where your property ended, and your neighbour's property began. It defined an undisputed position of certainty.

45 Rise

We just met.
With me now.
Black as jet.
Still, calm, warm,
impressive form.

Equine eye,
brown and clear.
Noble, proud,
reassuring air.

Nestling now.
Cheek by jowl.

Pulse of life,
embraces my soul.

Spirit stirs,
a new journey begins.

God wins.[42]

---

[42] The Montol Festival is a community event in Penzance that celebrates old Christian themes at the midwinter solstice.

Epilogue

*'One does not become
enlightened by imagining
figures of light,
but by making
the darkness conscious'*

– Carl Jung

Afterword

*"At some thoughts one stands perplexed,
above all at the sight of human sin,
and wonders whether to combat it by force
or by humble love.*

*Always decide
'I will combat it by humble love.'
If you resolve on that once and for all,
you can conquer the whole world.*

*Loving humility is a terrible force:
it is the strongest of all things,
and there is nothing else like it."*

– Fyodor Dostoevsky

'To win this war,
you must first claim
your peace'

#fearsmallLOVEBIG